Let's Begin!

Here are eight very different things. Let's point at each one and say its name.

A a — apple

B b — bee

C c — cat

G g — gorilla

H h — hat

I i — ice cream

M m — monkey

N n — necklace

O o — octopus

S s — strawberry

T t — train

U u — umbrella

Y y — yo-yo

Z z — zebra

D d	E e	F f
dog	elephant	fish
J j	K k	L l
jet	king	lamb
P p	Q q	R r
penguin	queen	rabbit
V v	W w	X x
violin	whale	xylophone

Trace the Letter A

To Parents: Provide a crayon and let your child trace the dotted lines. If they have difficulty, have your child trace the letter with their pointer finger, or hold their finger and help them trace the letter. After tracing, say, "A is for ant, alligator, and apple."

 Trace the A and say "A."

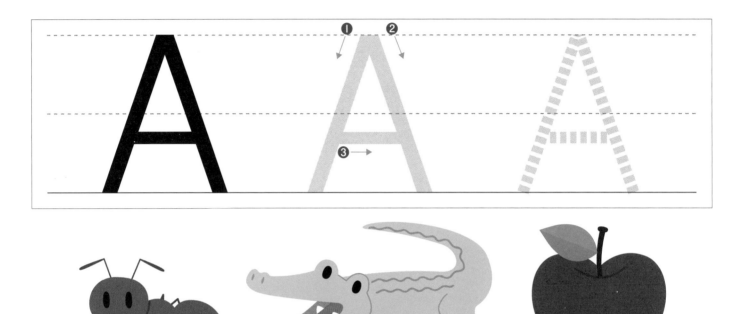

ant   alligator   apple

 Trace the lines from to .

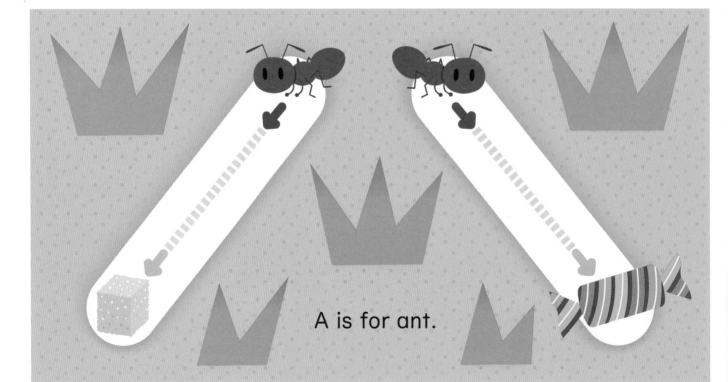

A is for ant.

Find the Letter A

To Parents: Cut along the solid gray lines. Then, give your child the alligators. Encourage them to use a glue stick on the backs of the alligators and try to place the alligators on the letter A. Together, say "A is for alligator." This activity helps builds fine motor skills.

 Glue two alligators where it says "paste." Then, find the letter A.

A a

example

paste   paste

A is for alligator.

Parents: Cut out the alligators for your child.

Trace the Letter B

To Parents: Provide a crayon and let your child trace the dotted lines. If they have difficulty, have your child trace the letter with their pointer finger, or hold their finger and help them trace the letter. After tracing, say, "B is for bee, balloon, and banana."

Trace the B and say "B."

B   B   B

bee   balloon   banana

Trace the lines from ➡ to ➡.

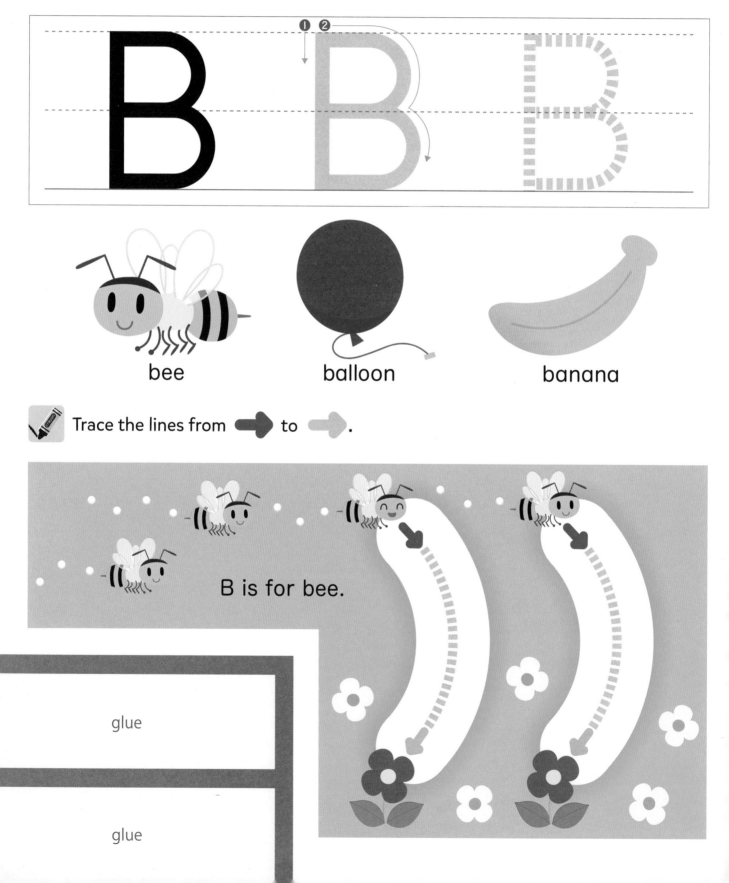

B is for bee.

glue

glue

Find the Letter B

To Parents: After saying "B is for balloon," ask your child to point to the red balloon, pick the matching crayon, and color the balloon. Do the same for the blue and pink balloons. Have your child circle the balloon shaped like a B to reinforce letter recognition.

 Color the balloons. Can you find the letter B?

B b

B is for balloon.

Trace the Letter C

To Parents: Provide a crayon and let your child trace the dotted line. If they have difficulty, have your child trace the letter with their pointer finger, or hold their finger and help them trace the letter. After tracing, say, "C is for cat, cow, and car."

Trace the C and say "C."

C   C   C

cat   cow   car

Trace the lines from ➡ to ➡.

C is for cat.

Find the Letter C

To Parents: Give your child stickers and ask them to decorate the cow in any way they choose. Decorating an object with stickers builds fine motor skills and encourages creativity.

Use stickers to give the cow spots. Then, find the letter C.

C c

Trace the Letter D

To Parents: Provide a crayon and let your child trace the dotted lines. If they have difficulty, have your child trace the letter with their pointer finger, or hold their finger and help them trace the letter. After tracing, say, "D is for duck, dog, and doughnut."

Trace the D and say "D."

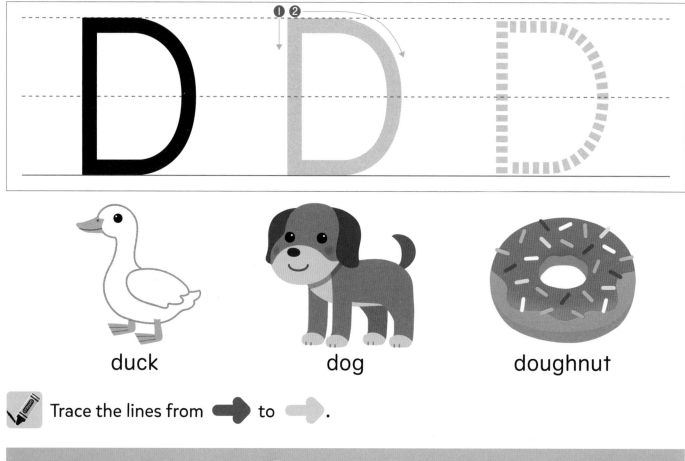

duck   dog   doughnut

Trace the lines from ➡ to ➡.

D is for duck.

Find the Letter D

To Parents: If your child is not sure how to draw the dog's face, help them by giving simple prompts to draw, such as the nose, mouth, and eyes. When the drawing is complete, say, "Dog and draw begin with D. We drew this dog together!"

 Draw a face on the dog. Can you find the letter D?

| D | d |

D is for dog.

example

Trace the Letter E

Trace the E and say "E."

envelope   elephant   eyes

Trace the lines from ➡ to ➡.

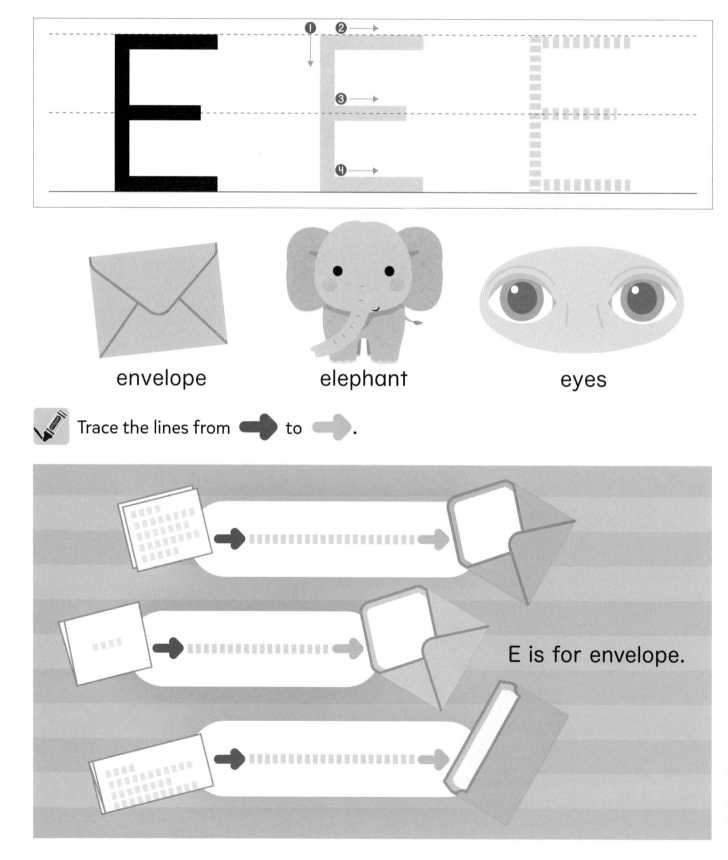

E is for envelope.

Find the Letter E

To Parents: Cut along the solid gray lines. Then, fold and crease along the dotted lines as shown to make a trunk for the elephant. Ask your child to put glue on the trunk and attach it to the elephant. Finally, trumpet like elephants together!

 Glue and place the trunk on the elephant. Can you find the letter E?

paste

How to Play

Fold

Paste

E is for elephant.

Parents: Cut out the trunk for your child.

Trace the Letter F

To Parents: Provide a crayon and let your child trace the dotted lines. If they have difficulty, have your child trace the letter with their pointer finger, or hold their finger and help them trace the letter. After tracing, say, "F is for fish, flower, and feet."

 Trace the F and say "F."

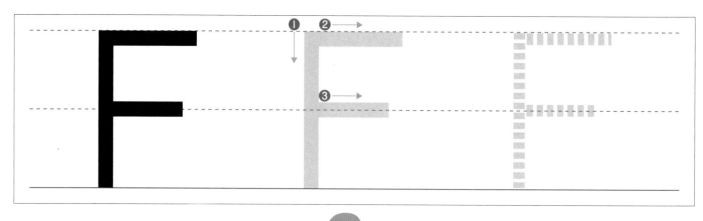

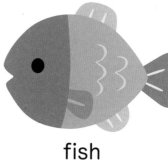

fish

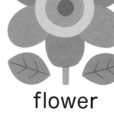

flower

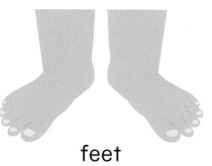

feet

 Trace the lines from ➡ to ➡.

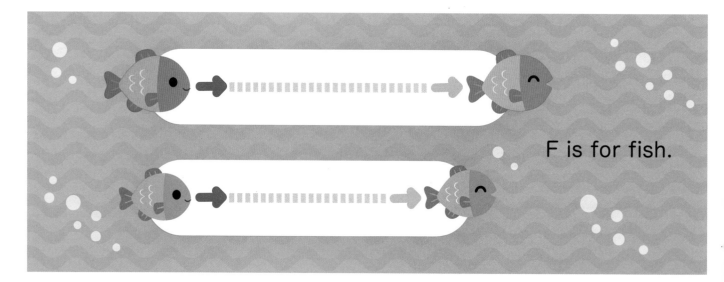

F is for fish.

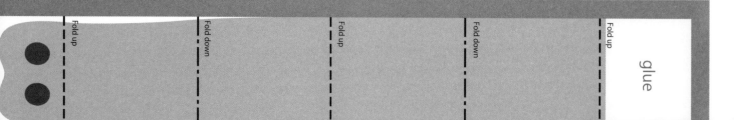

glue

Find the Letter F

To Parents: This activity focuses on observation skills to differentiate between various shapes and colors. Point out the example flower. Help your child begin to recognize the details that make things similar and different.

Point to all the pink flowers in this garden. Then, find the letter F.

| F | f |

example

F is for flower.

Uppercase & Lowercase A, B, C

To Parents: Help your child focus on the shapes of the objects in the left column, and ask them to point to the matching shadow shapes. Have your child draw lines to connect the matching pairs. Then, point out that the uppercase and lowercase letters are also matching pairs.

 Draw a line to connect each object with its shadow.

ant

example

A

a

banana

B

c

cat

C

b

Uppercase & Lowercase D, E, F

To Parents: Repeat the steps outlined on the previous page to connect each pair. Then, draw your child's attention to each set of uppercase and lowercase letters. (For example, say, "This is an uppercase D, and this is a lowercase d.")

Draw a line to connect each object with its shadow.

duck

envelope

flower

Trace the Letter G

To Parents: Provide a crayon and let your child trace the dotted lines. If they have difficulty, have your child trace the letter with their pointer finger, or hold their finger and help them trace the letter. After tracing, say, "G is for grasshopper, gorilla, and giraffe."

Trace the G and say "G."

G G G

grasshopper gorilla giraffe

Trace the lines from ➡ to ➡.

G is for grasshopper.

Find the Letter G

To Parents: As you point at each animal below, ask your child to say its name. Then, read the two "G is for . . ." sentences provided. Ask your child, "Which animal names begin with G?"

 Circle the two animals whose names begin with G. Then, find the letter G.

G is for gorilla.
G is for giraffe.

Sticker ★ Good job! ★

Trace the Letter H

To Parents: Provide a crayon and let your child trace the dotted lines. If they have difficulty, have your child trace the letter with their pointer finger, or hold their finger and help them trace the letter. After tracing, say, "H is for hat, hedgehog, and horse."

 Trace the H and say "H."

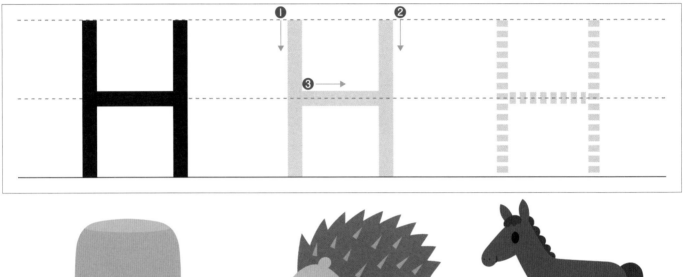

hat   hedgehog   horse

 Trace the lines from ➡ to ➡.

H is for hat.

Find the Letter H

To Parents: Grab two crayons: one for you, and one for your child. You can each make lines (in any color) to draw spines on the hedgehog. Then, encourage your child to name the hedgehog! Your involvement will increase your child's motivation.

 Draw spines on the hedgehog. Can you find the letter H?

H h

example

example

H is for hedgehog.

Trace the Letter I

To Parents: Provide a crayon and let your child trace the dotted lines. If they have difficulty, have your child trace the letter with their pointer finger, or hold their finger and help them trace the letter. After tracing, say, "I is for insects, ice cream, and island."

Trace the I and say "I."

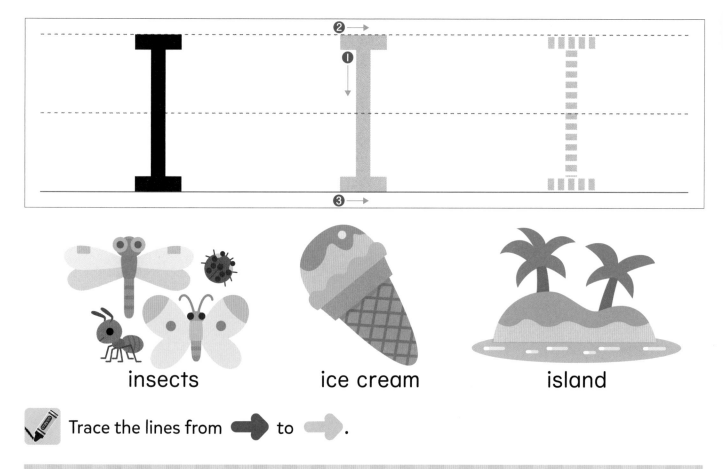

insects   ice cream   island

Trace the lines from ➡ to ➡.

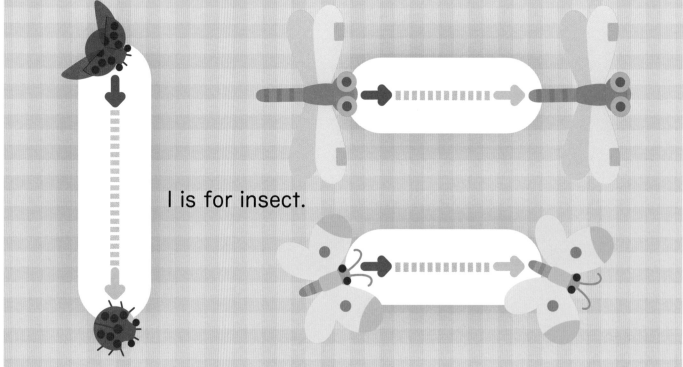

I is for insect.

Let's Scoop Ice Cream!

To Parents: Provide child-safe scissors and give your child the chance to cut out the ice cream below. They may glue the flavors in any order. When your child finishes, ask, "Which flavor do you like?"

 Cut out three ice cream flavors and paste them on top of the cone.

example

I is for ice cream.

paste

Trace the Letter J

To Parents: Provide a crayon and let your child trace the dotted line. If they have difficulty, have your child trace the letter with their pointer finger, or hold their finger and help them trace the letter. After tracing, say, "J is for jet, jellyfish, and jam."

Sticker
Good job!

Trace the J and say "J."

J   J   J

jet   jellyfish   jam

Trace the lines from ➡ to ➡.

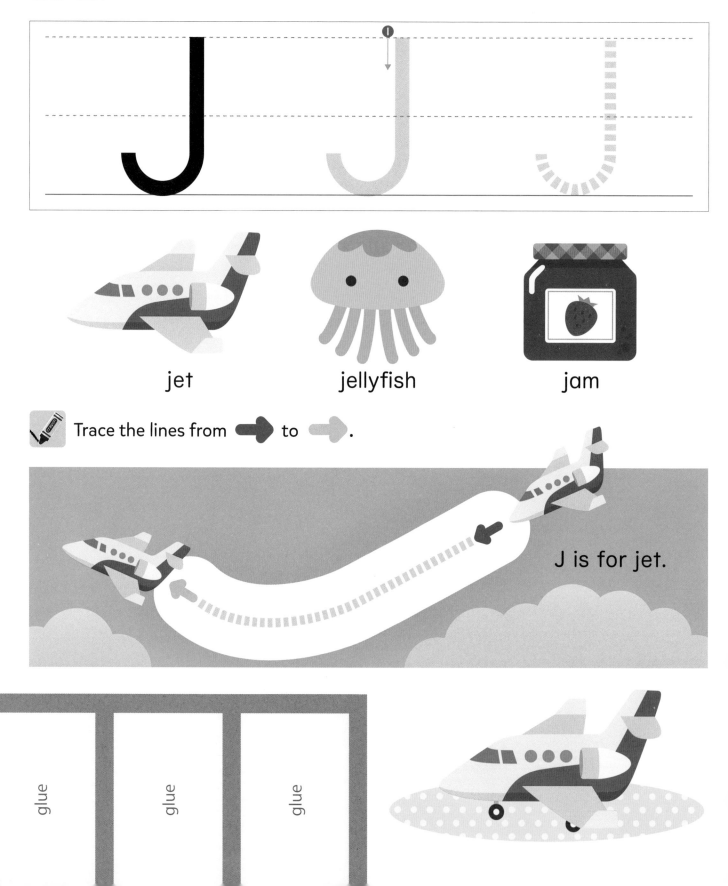

J is for jet.

glue   glue   glue

Find the Letter J

To Parents: Help your child practice matching a part with its whole. Call attention to details—such as shapes and colors—to help your child determine where each piece belongs. Repeat this activity so your child learns to spot similarities and differences more quickly.

J j

Draw a line to connect the images in the squares below to the matching animals in the picture. Find the letter J.

J is for jellyfish.

example

Trace the Letter K

To Parents: Provide a crayon and let your child trace the dotted lines. If they have difficulty, have your child trace the letter with their pointer finger, or hold their finger and help them trace the letter. After tracing, say, "K is for koala, king, and key."

Trace the K and say "K."

koala   king   key

Trace the lines from ➡ to ➡.

K is for koala.

Find the Letter K

To Parents: Say, "K is for key," as your child traces over each key in the maze.

K k

 Put the king sticker on its shadow below. Then, with your finger, guide the king to the K at the end of the maze without touching the walls. Collect four keys as you go!

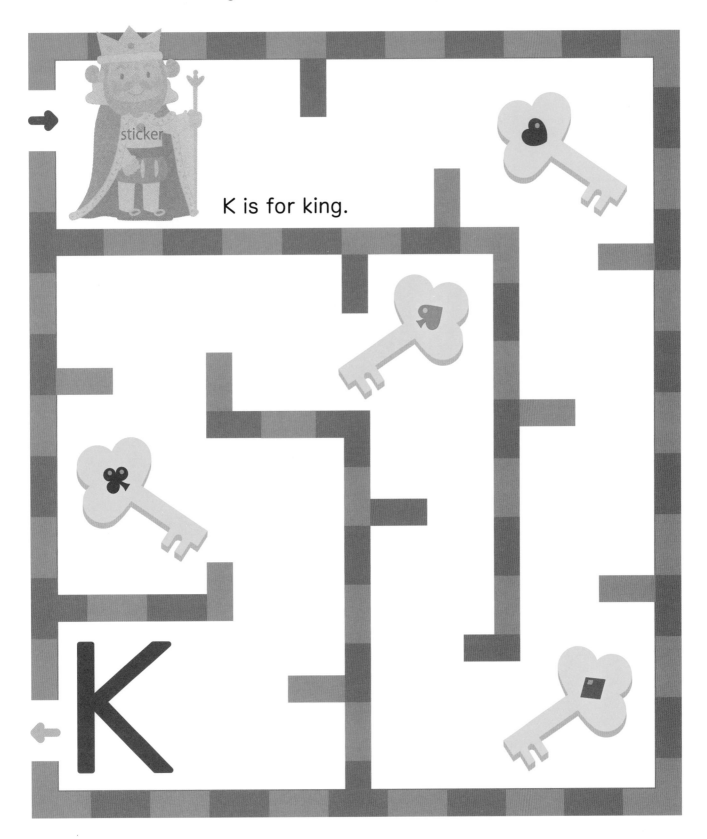

K is for king.

Trace the Letter L

 Trace the L and say "L."

ladybug   lamb   leaf

Trace the lines from ➡ to ➡.

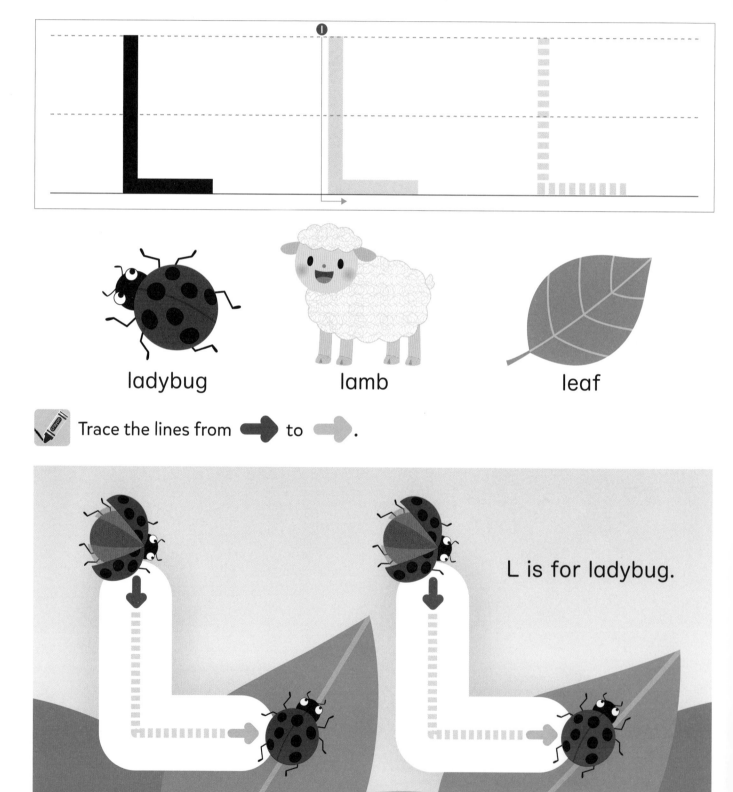

L is for ladybug.

Finish the Lamb

To Parents: Let your child tear the wool into small and large pieces. Now, encourage them to paste the pieces onto the lamb. After they finish, comment on their work. Tell them, "The lamb looks so soft and fluffy!"

 Cut out the wool at the bottom of the page. Tear it into pieces and paste them onto the lamb below.

L l

example

paste

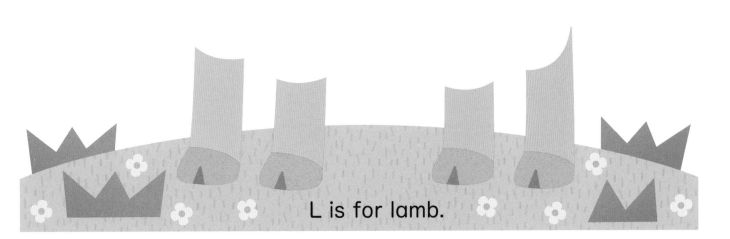

L is for lamb.

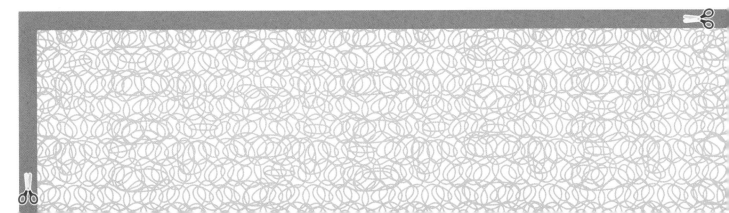

Sticker
★ Good job! ★

Uppercase & Lowercase G, H, I

To Parents: Help your child focus on the shapes of the objects in the left column, and ask them to point to the matching shadow shapes. Have your child draw lines to connect the matching pairs. Then, point out that the uppercase and lowercase letters are also matching pairs.

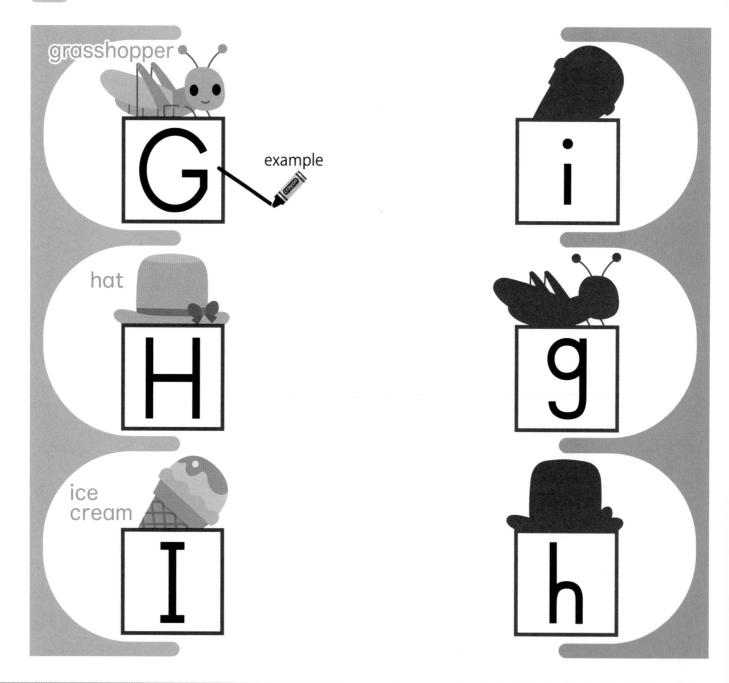

Draw a line to connect each object with its shadow.

grasshopper

G   example

hat

H

ice cream

I

i

g

h

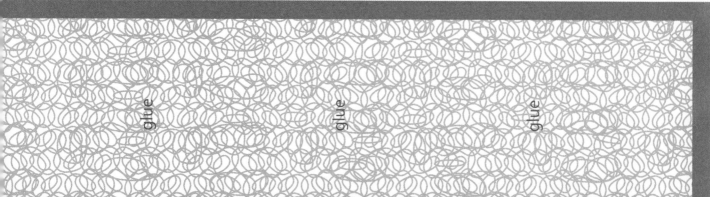

glue   glue   glue

Uppercase & Lowercase J, K, L

To Parents: Repeat the steps outlined on the previous page to connect the pairs. Then, draw your child's attention to each set of uppercase and lowercase letters. (For example, say, "This is an uppercase J, and this is a lowercase j.")

 Draw a line to connect each object with its shadow.

Trace the Letter M

To Parents: Provide a crayon and let your child trace the dotted lines. If they have difficulty, have your child trace the letter with their pointer finger, or hold their finger and help them trace the letter. After tracing, say, "M is for monkey, mouse, and moon."

Trace the M and say "M."

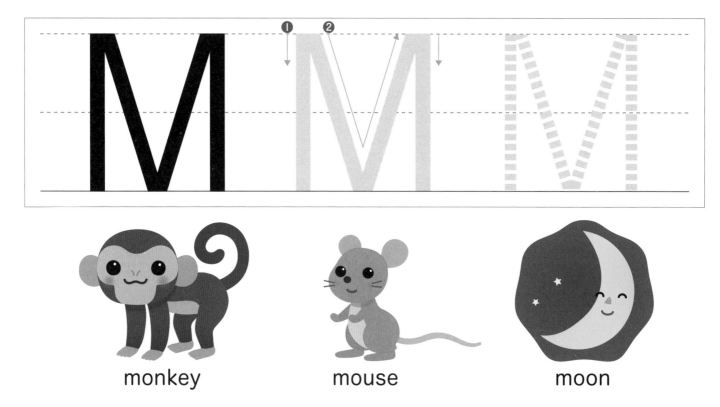

monkey   mouse   moon

 Trace the lines from ➡ to ➡.

M is for monkey.

Find the Letter M

To Parents: Give your child a crayon, and encourage them to follow the path without going outside the route. Say "M is for mouse," each time they pass over a mouse in the maze.

Trace a path from ➡ to ➡. Put three mouse stickers on the path.

M | m

M is for mouse.

sticker

sticker

sticker

Sticker

Good job!

Trace the Letter N

To Parents: Provide a crayon and let your child trace the dotted lines. If they have difficulty, have your child trace the letter with their pointer finger, or hold their finger and help them trace the letter. After tracing, say, "N is for nail, nest, and necklace."

 Trace the N and say "N."

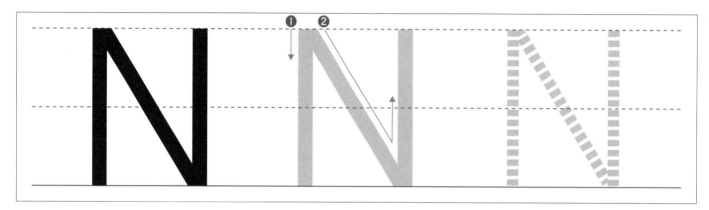

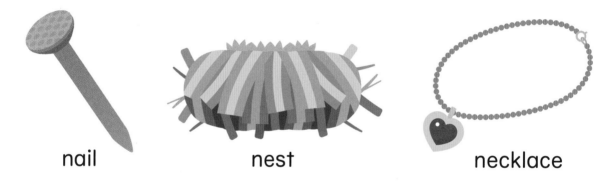

nail

nest

necklace

 Trace the lines from ➡ to ➡.

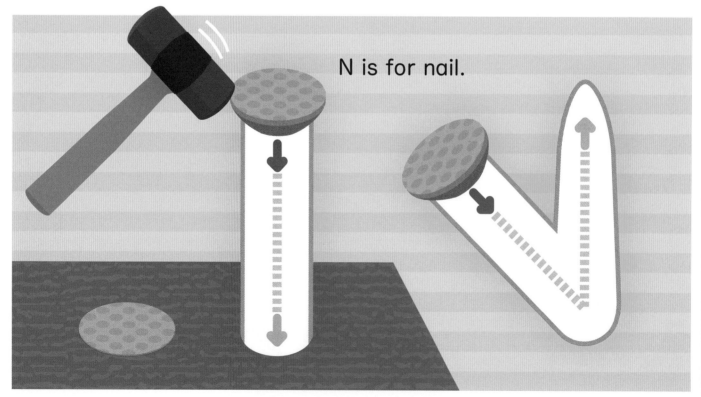

N is for nail.

Put Baby Birds in the Nest

To Parents: Provide child-safe scissors so your child can cut out the baby birds below. They do not need to glue the birds in the same order as they appear in the example.

Cut out the baby birds and paste them in the nest.

N n

N is for nest.

paste   paste   paste

N is for nest.

example

Trace the Letter O

To Parents: Provide a crayon and let your child trace the dotted line. If they have difficulty, have your child trace the letter with their pointer finger, or hold their finger and help them trace the letter. After tracing, say, "O is for octopus, onion, and orange."

 Trace the O and say "O."

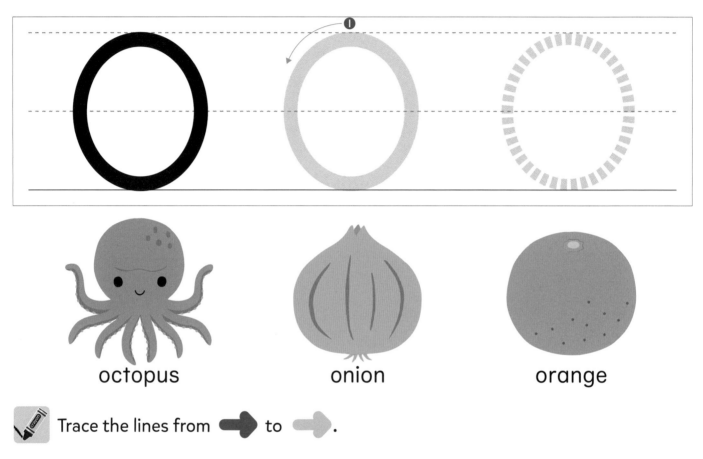

octopus   onion   orange

Trace the lines from ➡ to ➡.

O is for octopus.

glue   glue   glue

Which Begins with O?

To Parents: Before giving your child a crayon, say, "O is for orange" and "A is for apple." Then, ask your child, "O is for what?" Repetition helps build language recognition.

Circle the objects that start with the letter O.

O is for orange.

O is for octopus.

O is for onion.

Trace the Letter P

To Parents: Provide a crayon and let your child trace the dotted lines. If they have difficulty, have your child trace the letter with their pointer finger, or hold their finger and help them trace the letter. After tracing, say, "P is for penguin, pig, and panda."

 Trace the P and say "P."

P P P P

penguin   pig   panda

Trace the lines from ➡ to ➡.

P is for penguin.

Find the Letter P

To Parents: If your child is not sure how to draw the pig's face, help them by giving simple prompts to draw, such as the nose, mouth, and eyes. When the drawing is complete, say, "Pig and pink begin with P. We drew this pig together!"

Find and trace the letter P. Draw a face on the pig. Then, draw legs and a tail on the pig.

P | p

example

P is for pig.

Trace the Letter Q

To Parents: Provide a crayon and let your child trace the dotted lines on the page. If they have difficulty, have your child trace the letter with their pointer finger, or hold their finger and help them trace the letter. After tracing, say, "Q is for quail, queen, and quilt."

Trace the Q and say "Q."

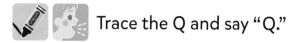

quail

queen

quilt

Trace the lines from ➡ to ➡.

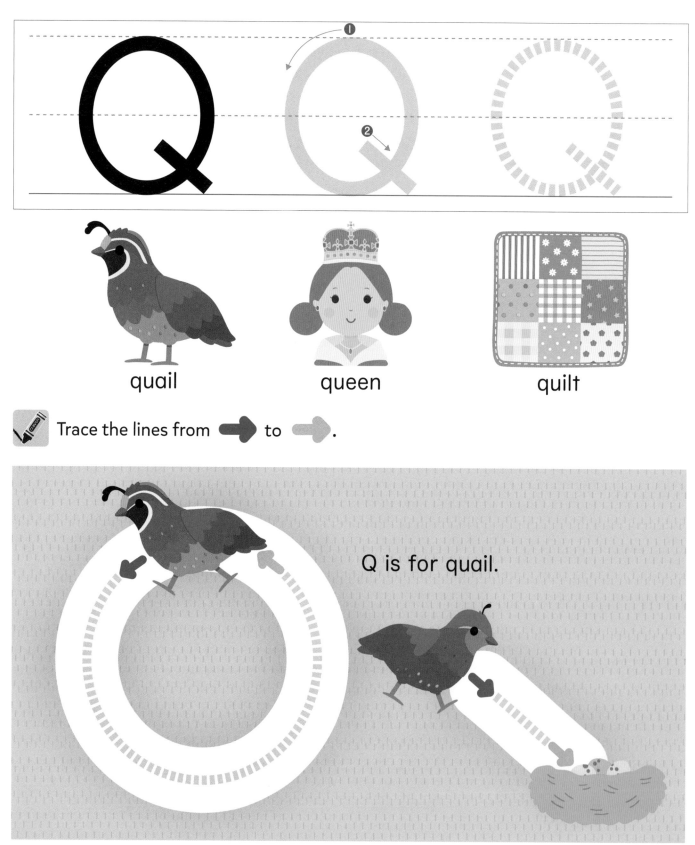

Q is for quail.

Go Through the Maze

To Parents: Say, "Q is for queen." Then, ask your child to point to a queen and say the word. Ask them to go through the maze, from one queen to the next, saying "queen" as they go. Finally, ask them how many queens there are.

Trace a path from ➡ to ➡ to meet all the queens.

| Q | q |

Q is for queen.

Trace the Letter R

To Parents: Provide a crayon and let your child trace the dotted lines. If they have difficulty, have your child trace the letter with their pointer finger, or hold their finger and help them trace the letter. After tracing, say, "R is for red, rainbow, and rabbit."

Trace the R and say "R."

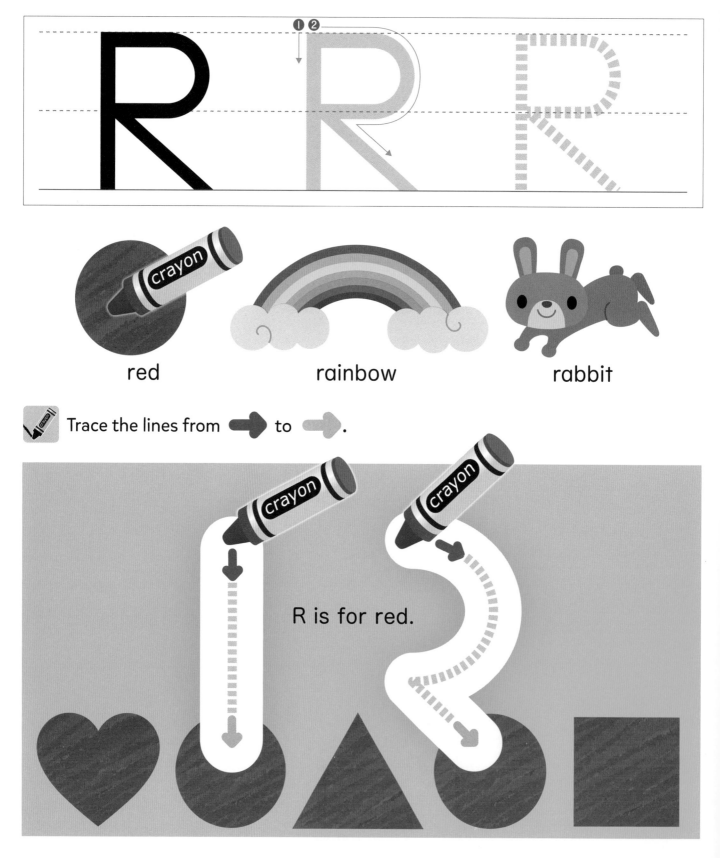

red   rainbow   rabbit

Trace the lines from ➡ to ➡.

R is for red.

Find the Letter R

To Parents: Provide child-safety scissors so your child can cut along the solid gray line. Then, let them fold and crease along the dotted lines. Each time they fold and unfold the page, say, "bear, rabbit, bear, rabbit." Say, "Rabbit begins with R."

Sticker
Good job!

 Cut and fold the page to discover the animal the rabbit turns into. Then, find the letter R.

 R r

R is for rainbow.

How to Play

Fold

Fold up

Fold down

Trace the Letter S

To Parents: Provide a crayon and let your child trace the dotted line. If they have difficulty, have your child trace the letter with their pointer finger, or hold their finger and help them trace the letter. After tracing, say, "S is for snake, ship, and strawberry."

 Trace the S and say "S."

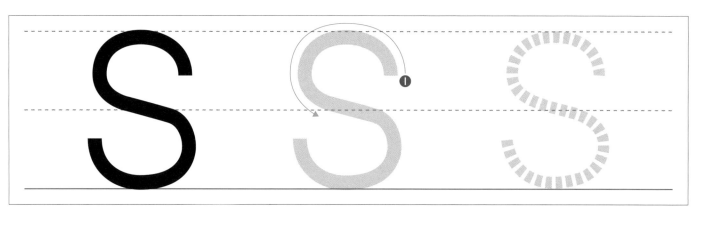

 snake ship strawberry

 Trace the lines from ➡ to ➡.

S is for snake.

Find the Letter S

To Parents: Encourage your child to put animal stickers on the squares provided in any order they choose. Then, give your child a crayon and ask them to trace the letter S.

Add animal stickers to the ship. Then, find and trace the letter S.

S s

S is for ship.

example

sticker   sticker   sticker

Sticker

Good job!

Uppercase & Lowercase M, N, O, P

To Parents: Help your child focus on the shapes of the illustrations, and ask them to point to the matching shadow shapes. Have your child draw lines to connect the matching pairs. Then, point out that the uppercase and lowercase letters are also matching pairs.

 Draw a line to connect each object with its shadow.

monkey

example

orange

nail

pig

Uppercase & Lowercase Q, R, S

To Parents: Repeat the steps outlined on the previous page to connect each pair. Then, draw your child's attention to each set of uppercase and lowercase letters. (For example, say, "This is an uppercase Q, and this is a lowercase q.")

 Draw a line to connect each object with its shadow.

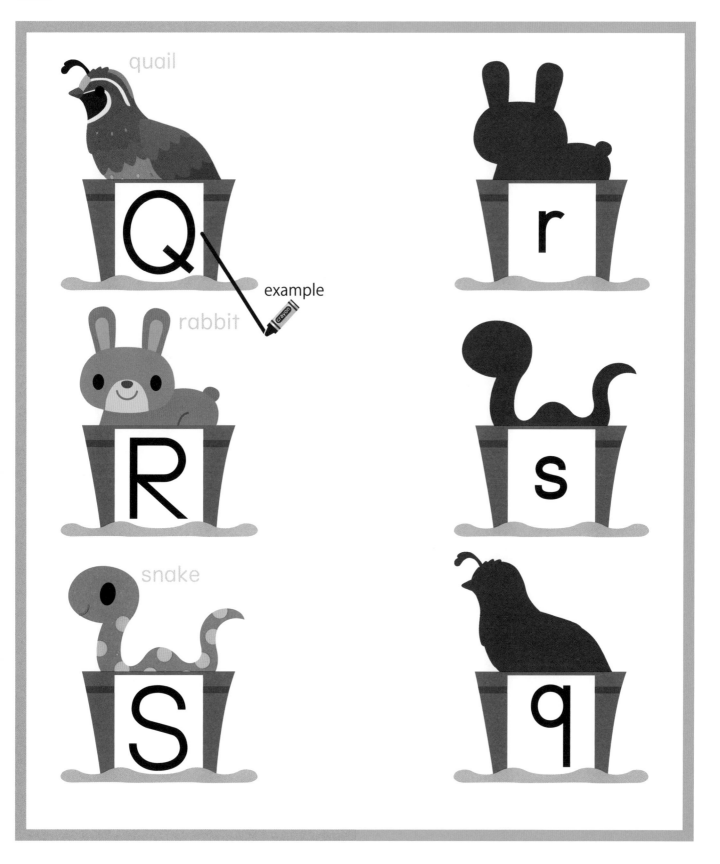

Trace the Letter T

To Parents: Provide a crayon and let your child trace the dotted lines. If they have difficulty, have your child trace the letter with their pointer finger, or hold their finger and help them trace the letter. After tracing, say, "T is for turtle, tiger, and train."

Trace the T and say "T."

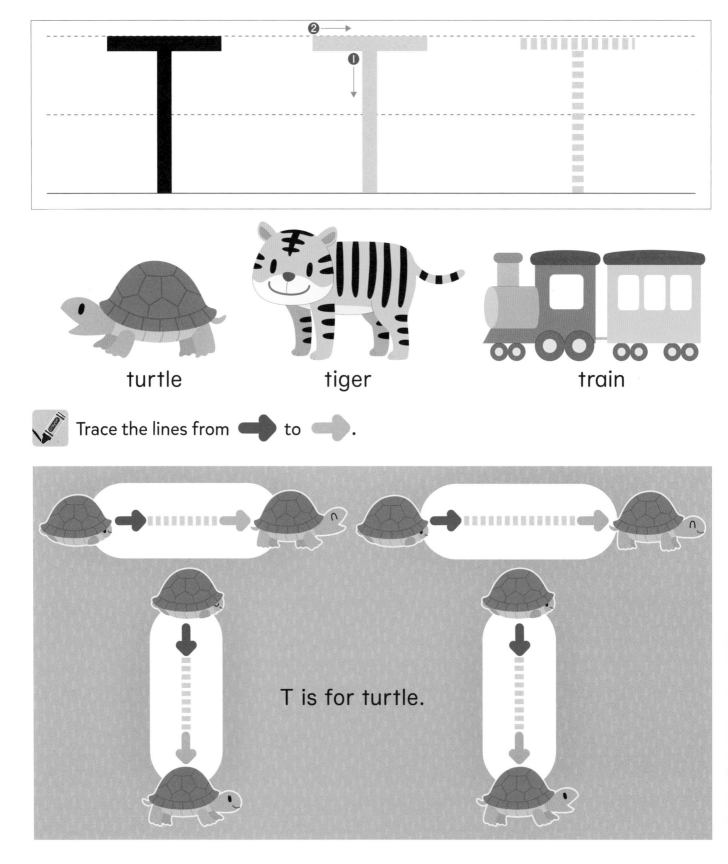

turtle   tiger   train

Trace the lines from ➡ to ➡.

T is for turtle.

Find the Letter T

To Parents: Encourage your child to find and trace the letter T with their finger. Then, ask them to trace the dotted lines with a crayon.

Good job!

 Find and trace the letter T. Then, color the tiger at the bottom of the page.

| T | t |

T is for tiger.

Trace the Letter U

To Parents: Provide a crayon and let your child trace the dotted line. If they have difficulty, have your child trace the letter with their pointer finger, or hold their finger and help them trace the letter. After tracing, say, "U is for unicorn, umbrella, and underwear."

 Trace the U and say "U."

unicorn

umbrella

underwear

 Trace the lines from ➡ to ➡ .

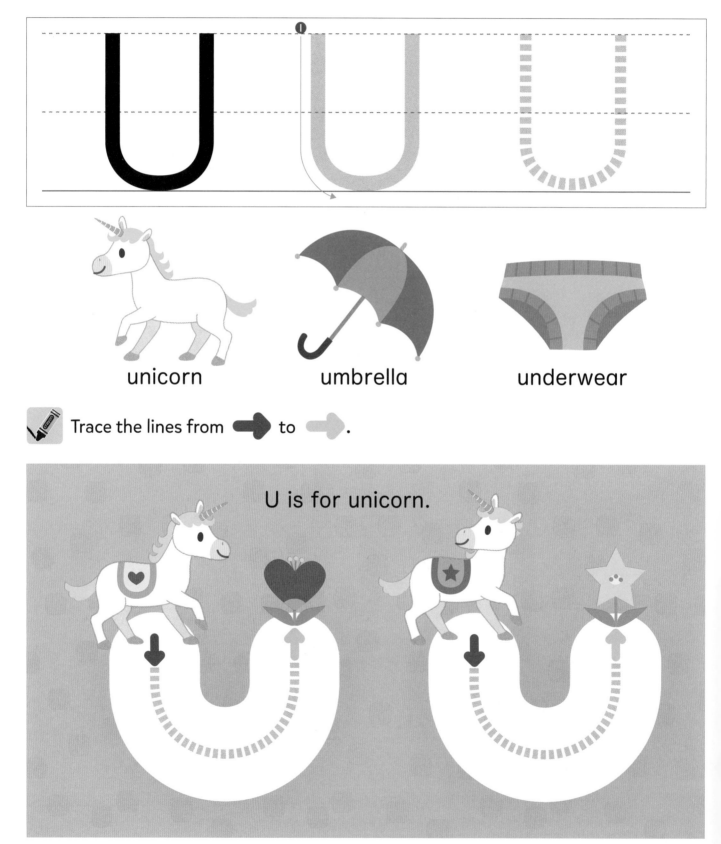

U is for unicorn.

Color the Umbrella

To Parents: Ask your child to point to the letter U in the coloring page below to practice recognizing letters. Then, ask your child to trace the outline of each section with a U. Now, ask them to color in the U sections in any color they choose and the other sections in blue. Finally, ask what the object is.

Sticker

★ Good job! ★

 Color the sections that contain a letter U. Then, name the object you've colored. Find the large letter U.

U u

U is for umbrella.

Trace the Letter V

To Parents: Provide a crayon and let your child trace the dotted lines on the page. If they have difficulty, have your child trace the letter with their pointer finger, or hold their finger and help them trace the letter. After tracing, say, "V is for vacuum, van, and violin."

Trace the V and say "V."

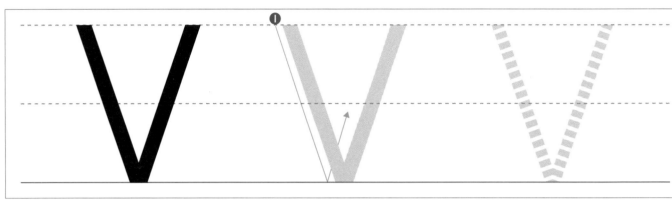

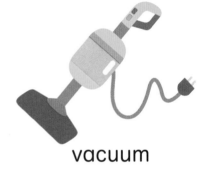

vacuum

van

violin

Trace the lines from ➡ to ➡.

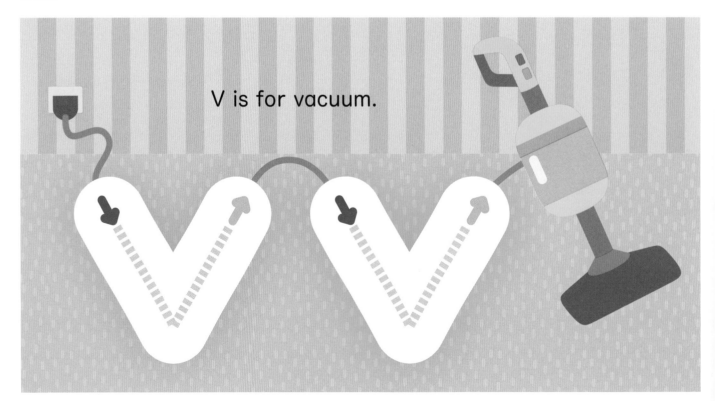

V is for vacuum.

Find the Letter V

To Parents: Let your child cut out and fold the van. Encourage them to say, "vroom, vroom," while moving the van along the road. Then, show your child that the van's path is in the shape of a V.

Cut out, fold, and make the van. Move the van along the V-shaped roads from  to .

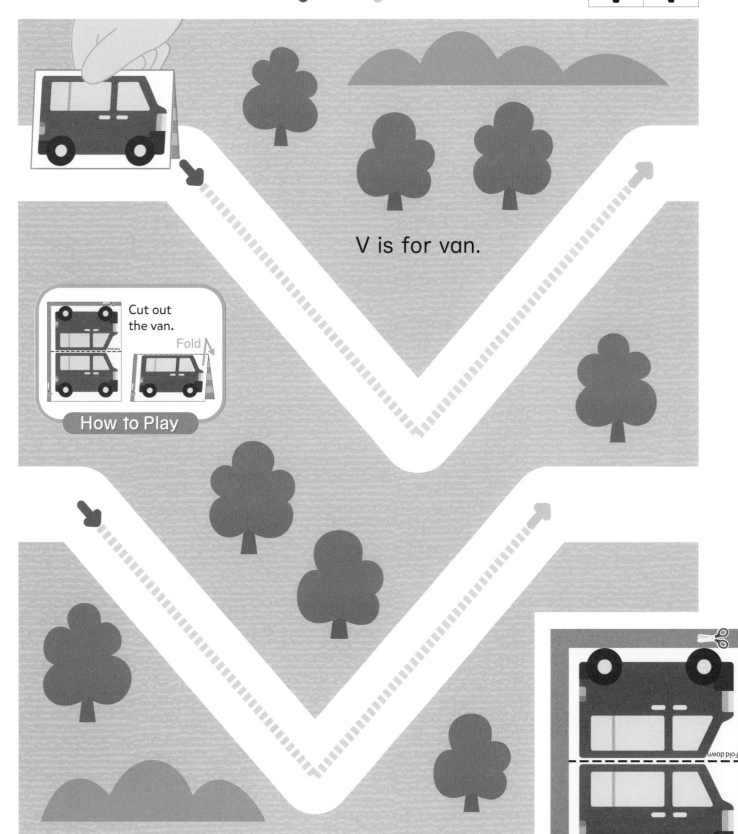

V is for van.

Cut out the van.

Fold

How to Play

Trace the Letter W

To Parents: Provide a crayon and let your child trace the dotted line. If they have difficulty, have your child trace the letter with their pointer finger, or hold their finger and help them trace the letter. After tracing, say, "W is for wolf, whale, and watermelon."

 Trace the W and say "W."

 wolf

 whale

 watermelon

 Trace the lines from ➡ to ➡.

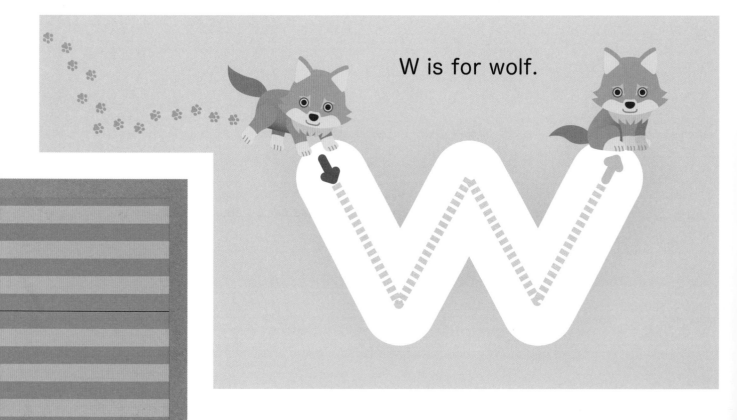

W is for wolf.

Find the Letter W

To Parents: If your child has difficulty connecting the dots, encourage them to connect only two dots at a time until the whole whale has been outlined.

Following the arrows, draw a line from ● to ○ and color the whale. Find and trace the letter W.

W is for whale.

example

Trace the Letter X

To Parents: Provide a crayon and let your child trace the dotted lines. If they have difficulty, have your child trace the letter with their pointer finger, or hold their finger and help them trace the letter. After tracing, say, "X is for xylophone, box, and X-ray."

 Trace the X and say "X."

xylophone   box   X-ray

Trace the lines from ➡ to ➡.

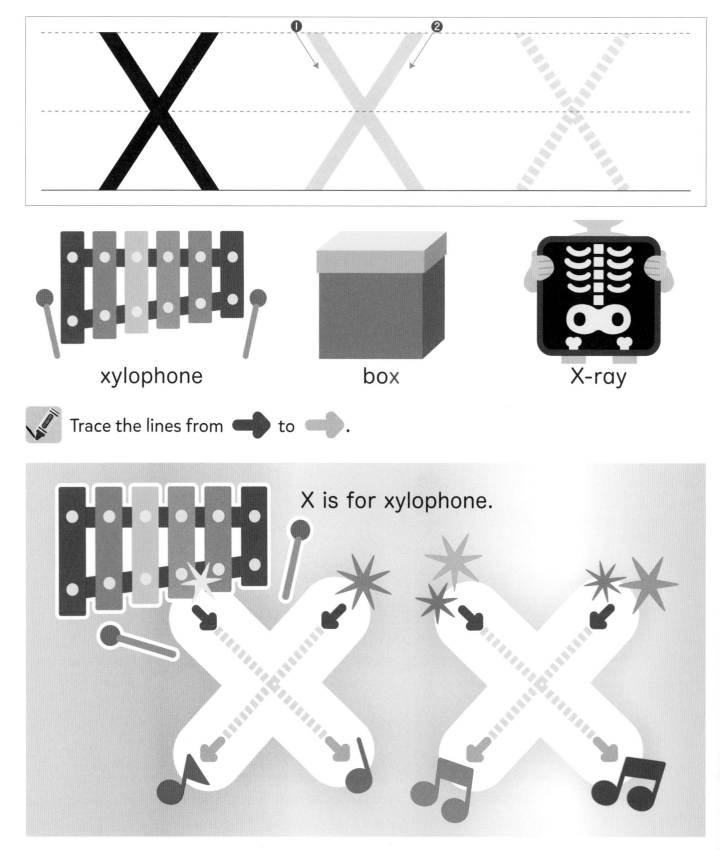

X is for xylophone.

Find the Letter X

To Parents: Ask your child to point to each X in the picture below. Provide a crayon and ask them to color in each box with an X on it. Then, encourage your child to color the rest of the boxes.

Find and color each box that contains the letter X.

| X | x |

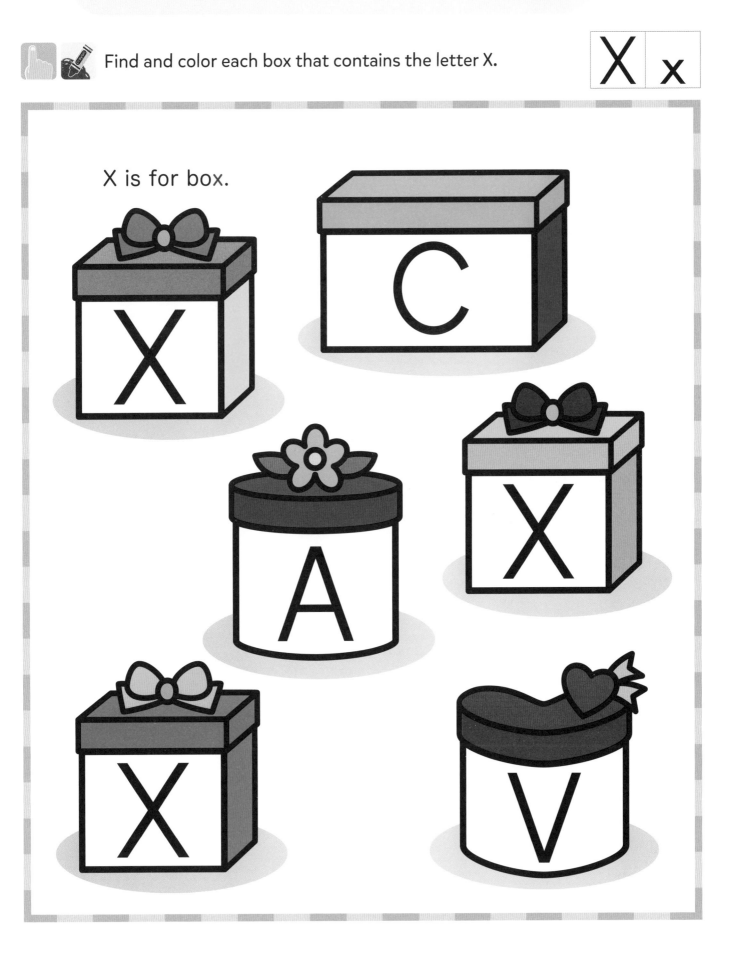

X is for box.

Trace the Letter Y

To Parents: Provide a crayon and let your child trace the dotted lines. If they have difficulty, have your child trace the letter with their pointer finger, or hold their finger and help them trace the letter. After tracing, say, "Y is for yellow, yarn, and yo-yo."

 Trace the Y and say "Y."

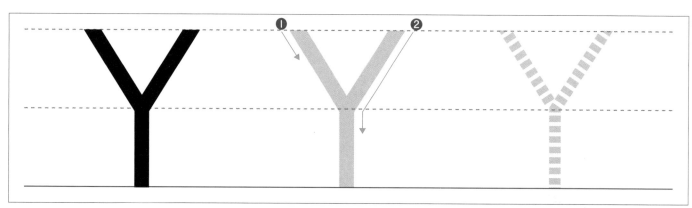

 yellow

 yarn

 yo-yo

 Trace the lines from ➡ to ➡.

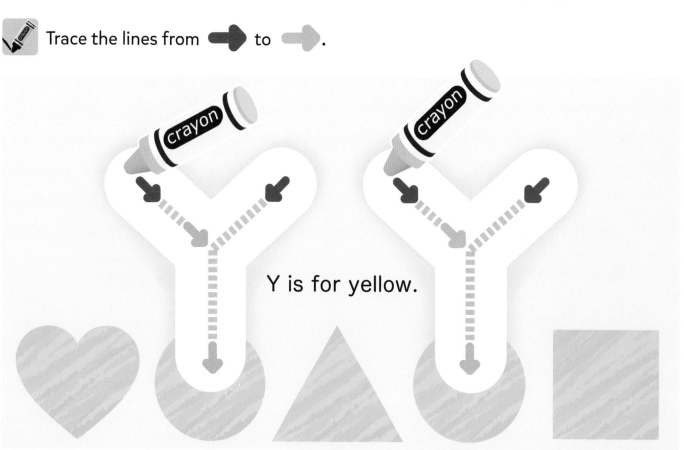

Y is for yellow.

Finish the Pattern

To Parents: Say, "yo-yo, yarn, yo-yo, yarn," to emphasize the pattern while pointing to the order of the objects. Then, ask your child to say it themselves. Finally, ask them to place the stickers in the same order on the page.

Trace the path from ➡ to ➡. Add the stickers to complete the pattern.

Y y

Y is for yo-yo.

Y is for yarn.

Trace the Letter Z

To Parents: Provide a crayon and let your child trace the dotted line. If they have difficulty, have your child trace the letter with their pointer finger, or hold their finger and help them trace the letter. After tracing, say, "Z is for zebra, zoo, and zipper."

Trace the Z and say "Z."

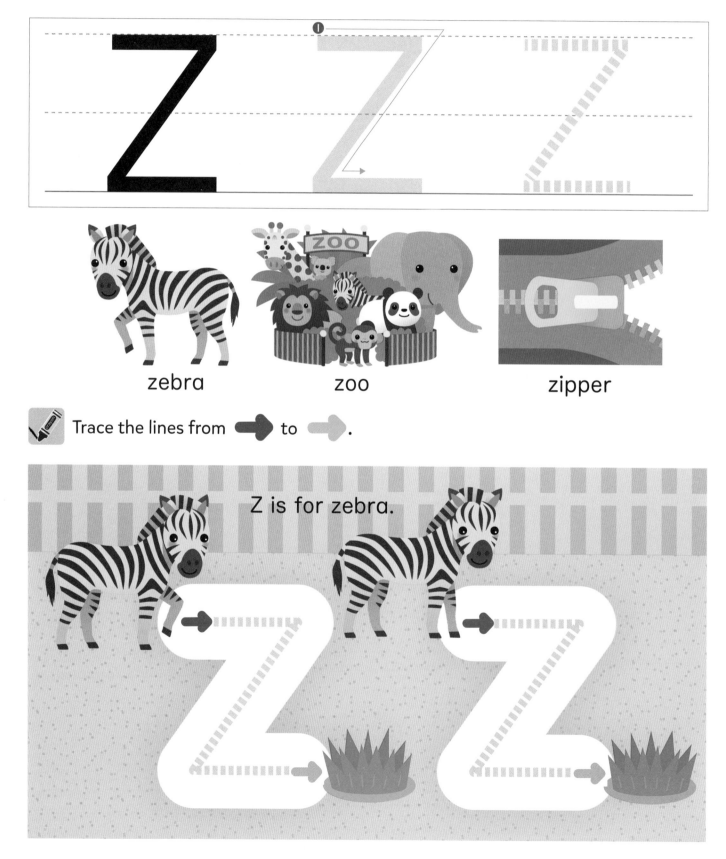

zebra   zoo   zipper

Trace the lines from ➡ to ➡.

Z is for zebra.

Spot the Differences

To Parents: In this activity, your child will practice finding differences between two similar pictures. Ask your child to look carefully at each picture. Provide hints, if needed. These are the items that are different in the bottom picture: flower, crow, bear, and zebra.

Find the four differences between the two pictures below. Put a **Z** sticker on each difference in the bottom picture.

Z | **z**

Z is for zoo.

Uppercase & Lowercase T, U, V, W

To Parents: Help your child focus on the shapes of the illustrations, and ask them to point to the matching shadow shapes. Have your child draw lines to connect the matching pairs. Then, point out that the uppercase and lowercase letters are also matching pairs.

 Draw a line to connect each object with its shadow.

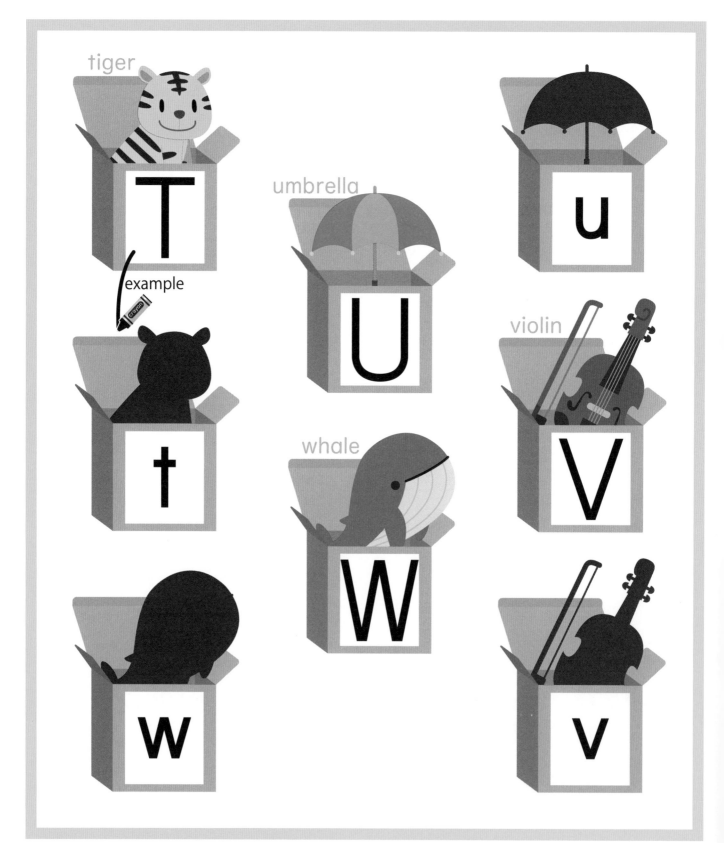

tiger

umbrella

u

T

U

example

violin

t

whale

V

W

W

v

Uppercase & Lowercase X, Y, Z

To Parents: Repeat the steps outlined on the previous page to connect each pair. Then, draw your child's attention to each set of uppercase and lowercase letters. (For example, say, "This is an uppercase X, and this is a lowercase x.")

 Draw a line to connect each object with its shadow.

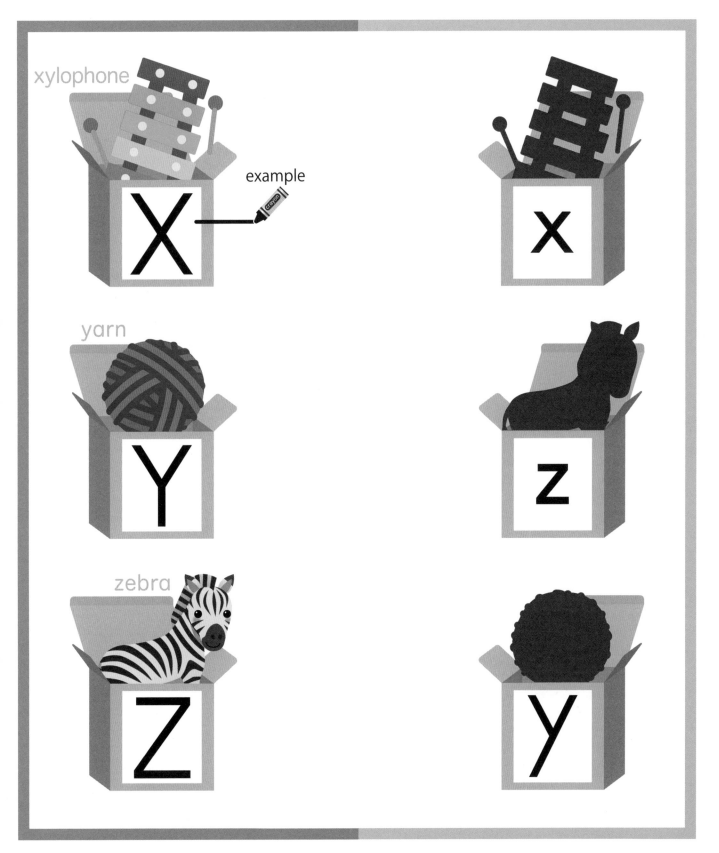

xylophone

example

yarn

zebra

Connect the Alphabet Dots

To Parents: Start by tracing the outline with your finger from dot to dot as you say the alphabet. Then, ask your child to do the same. Finally, provide a crayon and encourage your child to connect the dots—two at a time, if necessary.

Draw a line connecting the whole alphabet from A to Z. What do you see? Color the picture.

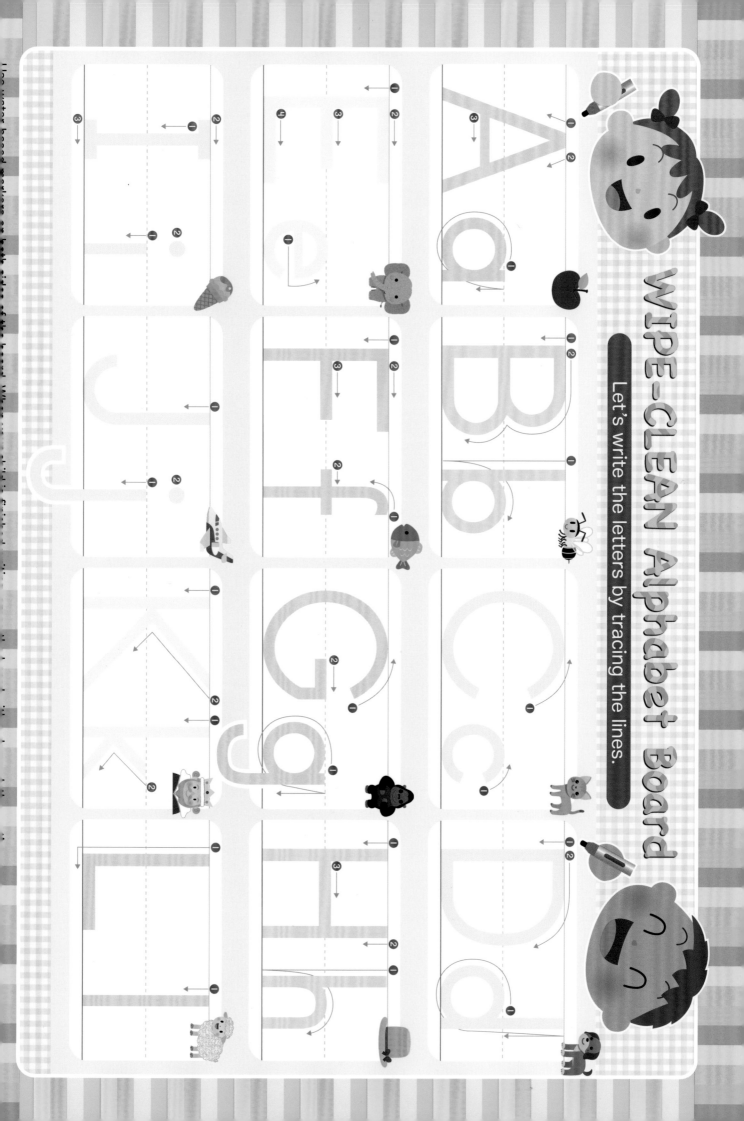

WIPE-CLEAN Alphabet Board

Let's write the letters by tracing the lines.

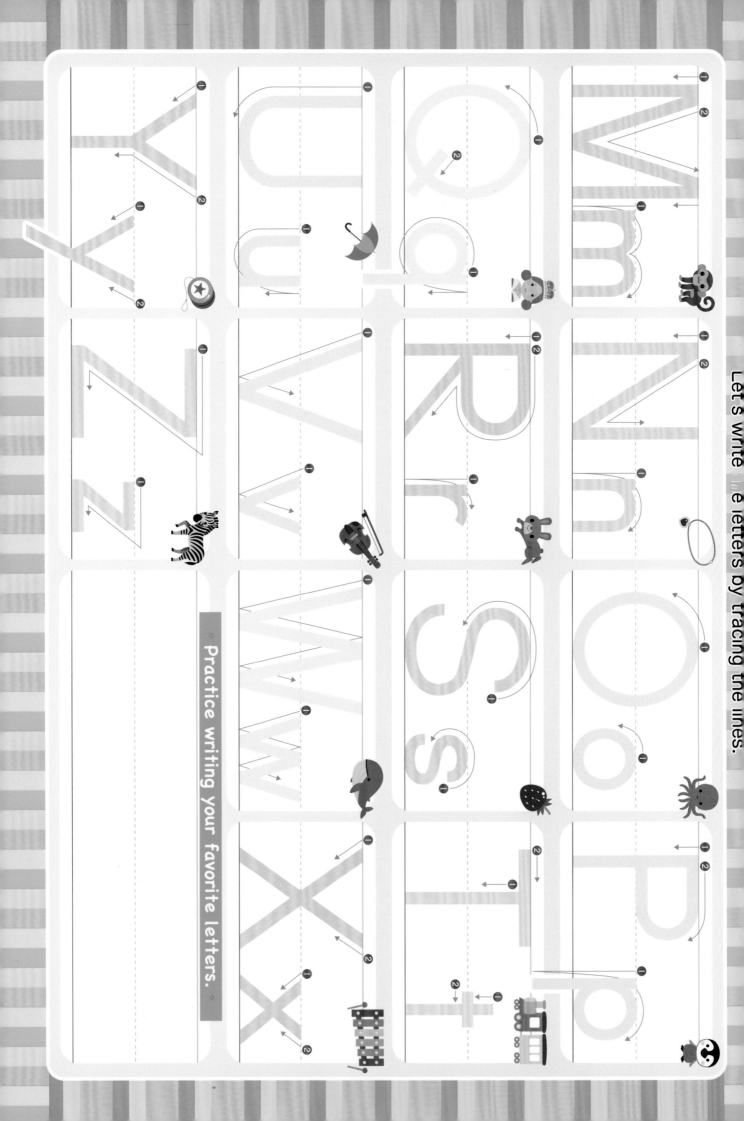

Practice writing your favorite letters.